START-UP
SCIENCE
MATERIALS

Claire Llewellyn

CHERRYTREE BOOKS

Distributed in the United States by
Cherrytree Books
1980 Lookout Drive
North Mankato, MN 56001

U.S. publication copyright © Cherrytree Books 2005
International copyright reserved in all countries. No part
of this book may be reproduced in any form without
written permission from the publisher.

Library of Congress Cataloging-in-Publication Data
applied for

First Edition
9 8 7 6 5 4 3 2 1

First published in 2004 by
Evans Brothers Limited
2A Portman Mansions
Chiltern Street
London W1U 6NR
Copyright © Evans Brothers Limited 2004

Conceived and produced by

White-Thomson Publishing Ltd.

Editor: Dereen Taylor
Consultants: Les Jones, Science Consultant, Manchester
Education Partnership; Norah Granger, former primary
school principal and senior lecturer in education,
University of Brighton.
Designer: Leishman Design

Picture Acknowledgments:
Chris Fairclough Colour Library 21;
Corbis 17 (top left), 18.
All other photographs by Chris Fairclough.

Printed in China

Acknowledgments:
Special thanks to the following for their help and
involvement in the preparation of this book: Staff and
pupils at Elm Grove Primary School, Liz
Price, family, and friends, Christine Clark and family.

Contents

All kinds of Materials

Tom and Olivia are having a picnic.

They are putting everything they need on a picnic table.

These objects are made of different materials.

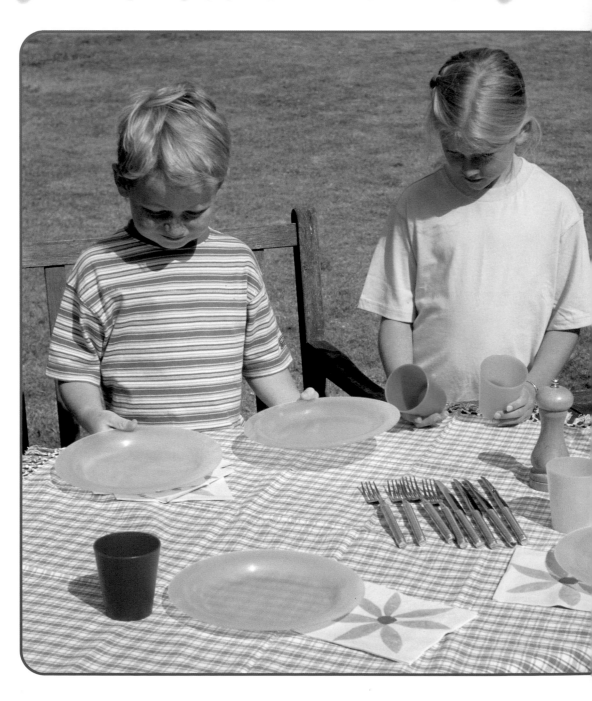

objects materials feel hard shiny

Each material has its own look and feel. Which ones are hard? Which ones are shiny?

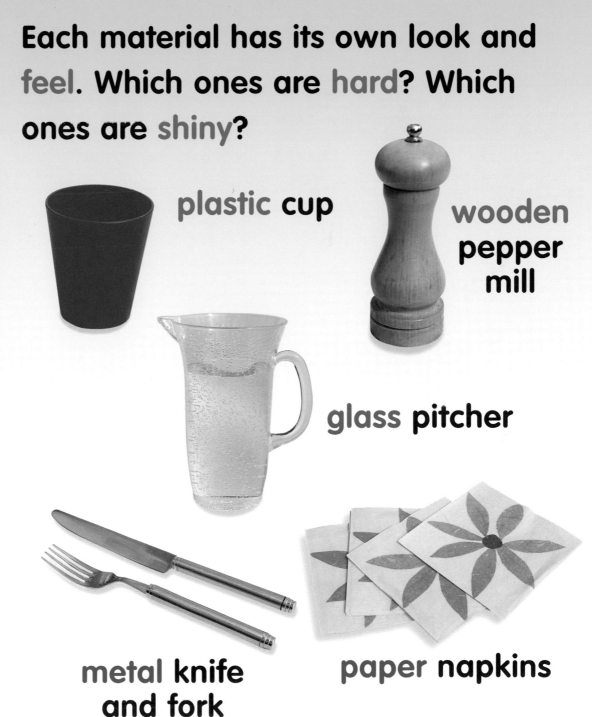

plastic **cup**

wooden **pepper mill**

glass **pitcher**

metal **knife and fork**

paper **napkins**

plastic   wooden   glass   metal   paper

Choosing Materials

► Clara is one year old. Her parents choose her things with care. They think about what materials they are made of.

The plastic tray on this highchair is strong and easy to clean.

Why do you think they chose a board book for Clara?

Why do you think they chose a fluffy teddy?

strong   easy   clean   board

When Clara eats, she wears a bib to protect her clothes from food. What kind of material makes a good bib?

▶ Ali is testing three different materials: paper, cloth, and plastic.

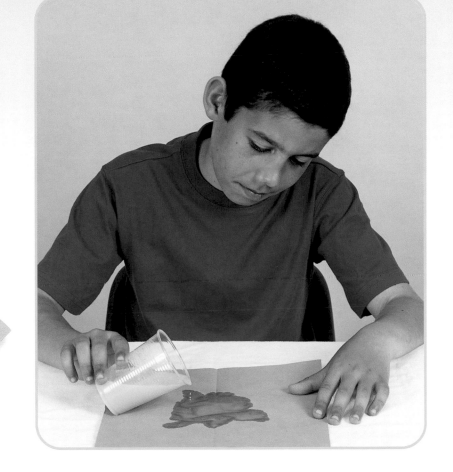

He puts each material on top of a white cloth, then he pours juice on each one in turn.

Which one do you think makes the best bib?

fluffy   protect   testing

Natural Materials

Justin is a carpenter. He works with wood. Wood comes from trees. It is a natural material. Natural materials are found in the world around us.

► Justin cuts the planks of wood on a saw.

wood   natural   world

◄ What did Justin have to do to the wood to make this door frame?

▼ Wood can also be used to make paper. You see tiny bits of wood in some kinds of paper.

cuts   planks

Building with Natural Materials

▶ **This house is made of bricks, stone, and wood.**

The bricks are made from clay, which is dug out of the ground.

Do you know where the stone comes from?

Bricks ••••••▶

Stone •••••

Wood ••••••••••••

bricks   stone   clay

Builders **choose materials that are strong and long-lasting.**

▲ Olivia wants to build a bridge over her train track.

▲ **Which of these materials would you choose to make a bridge?**

How would you make it?

Making Materials

Some materials are not natural. They are manufactured.

Plastic is not a natural material. It was invented by scientists, who made it out of oil.

There are hundreds of kinds of plastic. Each one looks and feels different, and is used for different things.

► These sunglasses use two different kinds of plastic.

hard and colorful plastic

see-through plastic

manufactured   scientists

strong   hard   soft

stretchy

waterproof

washable

light

colorful   bendy   spongy

Which of these words would you use to describe the plastic objects in the pictures? Can you think of any other things that are made of plastic?

oil   describe

Magnetic Materials

Magnets **have an** invisible **force that** pull things toward them.

▼ **Ernest tests his** magnet on things made of different materials.

Objects that can be picked up by a magnet are magnetic. **Magnetic objects are always made of metal.**

magnets force magnetic

▲ See how many metal objects you can pick up with a magnet.

Not everything made of metal is magnetic.

► Look at the cans in the picture. What does the magnet tell us about them?

Changing Shape

◄ Charmaine is blowing up a balloon. The balloon is changing shape. It stretches as it fills with air.

What will happen when Charmaine lets the air out?

Some materials hold a new shape. Others spring back when you let them go.

changing shape stretches

◄ **Keith is making a mug out of clay.**

He squishes and bends the clay until it is the right shape.

► **We can change the shape of many materials. What could you do to these objects to change their shape?**

hold spring back squishes bends **17**
......

Heat Changes Things

▶ Keith's clay mug is not very strong. He puts it into an **oven** called a kiln. The oven's **heat hardens** the clay and makes the mug **stronger**.

Heat can change some materials. Changes like this often last forever. You cannot change them back.

Cooking is a way of changing some foods, making them **safer** to eat.

⚡WARNING!
Ovens are dangerous.
Never cook by yourself.

oven   heat   hardens

▶ Make a chart
to compare
each of these
foods before
and after
cooking.

Food	Before cooking	After cooking
Pasta	hard, brittle, not good to eat	Soft, squishy, good to eat
Eggs		
Sausages		

stronger cooking safer soft

Cooling Materials

▶ Rosie is making popsicles. She pours fruit juice into the molds. Then she puts them in the freezer.

◀ Three hours later, she takes one out. How has the fruit juice changed? What other things change when you put them in the freezer?

popsicles pours molds freezer

Many materials change as they cool. Look at the two pictures.

◀ What does the gelatin look like when it is hot?

▶ What does it look like when it is cold?

cool   hot   cold

Further Information for

New words listed in the text:

bends	cooking	freezer	magnetic	oil	safer	stretches
board	cool	glass	magnets	oven	scientists	strong
bricks	cuts	hard	manufactured	paper	shape	stronger
builders	describe	hardens	materials	planks	shiny	testing
changing	easy	heat	metal	plastic	soft	wood
clay	feel	hold	molds	popsicles	spring back	wooden
clean	fluffy	hot	natural	pours	squishes	world
cold	force	long-lasting	objects	protect	stone	

Possible Activities

PAGES 4–5

Make a collection of objects made from many different materials. Label them.

Ask children to identify objects (e.g. wooden beads, metal key, soap) with their eyes closed. How do they manage to do this?

PAGES 6–7

Make a puppet using different materials. Draw a picture of the puppet, labeling the materials and explaining why they were chosen (e.g. "I used wool for the hair because it is long and stringy.")

Ask the children to make a greeting card. Think what kind of paper/cardboard will be most suitable for the job. Why? Test out their ideas.

PAGES 8–9

Make a display of wooden materials. Use reference books or CDs to find out more about the uses of wood.

PAGES 10–11

Collect pictures of natural materials and the products they are used to make (e.g. sheep's wool/a woolen scarf; reeds/ thatched roof). Can children match the material to the product?

Ask children to make a toy slide. What kind of materials would be suitable and why? Get them to test their ideas.

PAGES 12–13

Make a collection of plastic objects. Group and label them according to their characteristics.

Make a collection of items made of paper, such as tissue paper, cardboard, paper towel, etc. What words describe the different kinds of paper? Now sort the items into different groups.

PAGES 14–15

Make a collection of different kinds of magnets.

Make a magnetic fishing game with fish cut out of foil and a fishing rod made of a stick, some string, and a magnet.

Parents and Teachers

Slide paper clips onto the fish and drop them in a bowl of water. How many can you catch?

PAGES 16–17

Ask children to collect a number of objects (e.g. a towel, a banana, a stone) and test whether they will stretch, bend, squash, or twist. Compile the results on a chart.

Explore the properties of rubber bands, foam sponges, and soft rubber balls. What happens when you squash and stretch these?

PAGES 18–19

Give children the ingredients for scones to mix. Bake them and look at the finished scones together. Can the children describe the differences they observe before and after heating?

Why do we boil eggs? Show children a raw and a hard-boiled egg. Discuss the differences between them.

Discuss which foods we eat raw and which we eat cooked. Why do we cook some foods and not others?

PAGES 20–21

Make some ice cubes in the freezer. Now leave them out around the classroom. How long do they take to melt? Which ones melt first and why?

Make some crispy cakes by stirring cornflakes into some melted chocolate and spooning the mixture into paper cases. What happens as they cool?

Glass hardens as it cools. Use a reference book to find out how glass objects are made.

Further Information

BOOKS FOR CHILDREN

Godwin, Sam. *All Kinds of Everything.* Mankato, MN: Smart Apple Media, 2002.

Madgwick, Wendy. *Science Starters: Super Materials.* Chicago: Raintree, 2002.

Pluckrose, Henry. *Find Out About* series. London: Franklin Watts, 2002.

Riley, Peter. *Ways Into Science: Changing Materials/Materials.* London: Franklin Watts, 2001.

Hewitt, Sally. *Why Can't I Sleep on a Bed of Bubbles? and Other Questions about Materials.* London: Belitha Press, 2001.

BOOKS FOR ADULTS

Huns, Monica. *How to Sparkle at Science Investigations.* Dunstable, UK: Brilliant Publications.

WEB SITES

www.howstuffworks.com

www.niehs.nig.gov/kids/links.htm

www.sciencemaster.com

Index